MARC-ANTOINE CHARPE

Te Deum

H.146

for SATB chorus, soloists and orchestra

Edited by/Édité par/Herausgegeben von

LIONEL SAWKINS

VOCAL SCORE/PARTITION RÉDUITE/
KLAVIERAUSZUG

Contents · Table · Inhalt

FABER ff MUSIC

Orchestra/Orchestre/Orchester

Trumpet(s)/Trompette(s)/Trompete(n)

Bass trumpet (or Trombone)/Basse de trompette (ou Trombone)/
Baßtrompete (oder Posaune)

Timpani/Timbales/Pauken

2 Flutes or Recorders/2 Flûtes ou Flûtes à bec/
2 Flöten oder Blockflöten

2 Oboes/2 Hautbois/2 Oboen

Violins/Violons/Violinen

Violas 1 & 2/Altos 1 et 2/Viola 1 & 2

Bass violins (or Cellos)/Basses de violon (ou Violoncelles)/
Basses de violon (oder Violoncelli)

Bassoons/Bassons/Fagotten

Continuo:
Organ (manuals)/Orgue (clavier)/Orgel (Manuals)
Bass violin (or Cello)/Basse de violon (ou Violoncelle)/Basse de violon (oder Violoncello)
Theorbo(s)/Théorbe(s)/Theorb(en)

Duration: *c.*22 minutes

Full Score available on sale (ISBN 0-571-51376-X)
Parts available on hire

Lionel Sawkins's edition of Charpentier's *Te Deum* is recorded by
the St James's Singers and the St James's Baroque Players
conducted by Ivor Bolton on Teldec 0630-12465-2

This edition © 1996 by Faber Music Ltd
First published in 1996 by Faber Music Ltd
3 Queen Square London WC1N 3AU
Cover design by S & M Tucker
French translations by Marc Desmet
German translations by Eva Zöllner
Music processed by Lionel Sawkins
Printed in England by Caligraving Ltd
All rights reserved

ISBN 0-571-51375-1

To buy Faber Music publications or to find out about the full range of titles available
please contact your local music retailer or Faber Music sales enquiries:

Faber Music Limited, Burnt Mill, Elizabeth Way, Harlow, CM20 2HX England
Tel: +44 (0)1279 82 89 82   Fax: +44 (0)1279 82 89 83
sales@fabermusic.com   www.fabermusic.com

Preface

The *Te Deum* in D major (H.146) probably dates from Charpentier's last years, either when he was *maître de musique* for the Jesuits in Paris (in the early 1690s) or later (1698-1704) when he held a similar post at La Sainte-Chapelle; here he was responsible for the music for many ceremonial occasions. It is presented here for the first time in an edition which rigorously follows his intentions, explicitly set out in the clear calligraphy of his autograph score.

This setting, with its 'royal' additions of trumpets and timpani, was clearly following a trend established by Lully's version of 1677 and Lalande's of 1684 and must also have been closely contemporary with Purcell's of 1694. Such works were almost always designed to adorn royal celebrations of thanksgiving. The most obvious difference between the festive settings of Charpentier's contemporaries and his own is the latter's brevity, and this concise approach may have influenced Lalande to reduce his earlier work to half its previous dimensions by 1706; from much the same time, examples of some part-books of the 1684 printed edition of Lully's *Te Deum* also show substantial cuts made by the royal copyist, André Danican Philidor *l'aîné*.

Vocal Scoring

Although five soloists are sufficient – two *dessus* (soprano), *haute-contre* (high tenor or alto), *taille* (tenor), and *basse* (bass) – Charpentier actually calls for a vocal *petit chœur* of eight singers, two of each voice, with a *grand chœur* in the same four parts. (It is probable that even this larger group only contained some three or four singers per part at La Sainte-Chapelle in Charpentier's day.) In this edition, *haute-contre* parts are notated in treble clef to assist where these parts will be sung by counter-tenors or altos; nonetheless, where possible, tenors should be employed for the solo *haute-contre* lines, and preferably also in the chorus, matching the tone quality that Charpentier must have had in mind. (Quite apart from this difference in tone quality, *haute-contre* parts in French baroque music often pass below the serviceable range of many male or female altos, especially when performed at the lower pitch employed in Charpentier's day; see 'Other performance considerations' below.)

Keyboard reduction

The keyboard reduction is cued with changes in orchestration to assist in performances accompanied by organ alone where no orchestra is available. Small notes in the keyboard reduction indicate editorial realisation of the figuring. It should also be remembered that the French organ at this time only had 8' pitches available on the pedals, and 16' pitch was therefore not used for the organ bass, any more than it was present in the orchestra where the lowest-pitch instrument was the bass violin (tuned a tone lower than the cello).

Editorial procedure

Clefs and nomenclature. The original clefs are shown in the Full Score in *incipits* the first time each particular vocal or instrumental line appears. The key and time signatures employed by Charpentier are preserved. The latter have significant tempo connotations (see below: 'Tempo and tempo relationships') and to modernise them would hide these associations. In the Full Score, all of Charpentier's rubrics have been retained (always shown in roman type), and expanded where necessary, such expansions being included in square brackets (in the Vocal Score the brackets are omitted, and varying styles of nomenclature have been standardised; the original indications can always be found by consulting the Full Score). Editorial translations or interpretations for English-speaking readers are shown in *italics*; those for German readers are in roman. Editorial footnotes are given first in italics to distinguish them from Charpentier's instructions, which are given first in roman type in each case.

In both vocal and instrumental lines, Charpentier alternates solo indications with the direction 'Tous' (tutti). The bass line is marked alternately 'Tous' and 'Acc[ompagnement] seul', the latter employed in the accompaniment of solos or ensembles and corresponding to *basse-continue*, that is to say, only the instruments of the continuo, which here means organ, bass viol (or bass violin/cello) and theorbo.

In the Vocal Score, to avoid confusion with the general directions for singers (printed 'TOUS') these alternating instructions to the bass are printed immediately above the figured bass line (the left hand of the keyboard reduction) in lower case, 'tous', alternating with 'acc. seul'.

Tempo and tempo relationships. Charpentier numbered bars throughout the work in one sequence, indicating every hundredth bar, thus implicitly underlining the integrity of the repeat sequence in the opening *rondeau*. However, the numbering of movements is editorial, and for convenience in rehearsal only; it is not meant to imply any separation into movements in performance, although, as will be quickly seen, there are several places where Charpentier specifically calls for a pause of longer or shorter duration. The very fact that he felt it necessary to spell this out reminds us of the normal Baroque practice of playing such works continuously from 'movement' to 'movement', a practice Charpentier sometimes underlines with rubrics enjoining performers to move on without delay between movements e.g., 'passez sans interruption à la suite' ('continue without interruption to the next movement').

The existence of this practice also reminds us of the necessity of considering the relationship between the tempo of one 'movement' and the next, and such relationships would have been based on the traditions of the old mensural system with which all seventeenth-century musicians were familiar, where different time-signatures operated in proportion to one another. Although it is not always clear what exact proportions Charpentier had in mind, in this work or in others, the editor has taken the liberty of suggesting likely tempo relationships, based on evidence from other works of the period for which notated timings exist, and from theoretical treatises widely available at the time. The basic principles of these relationships may be summed up as follows:

(i) ♩ of **C** = ♩ of **¢** or 2

(ii) for most composers and theorists in France (as in England) 2 was the fastest tempo and often twice the speed of **¢**; however, for some, and Charpentier was evidently among them, the reverse seems sometimes to have been the case, with **¢** the fastest tempo, as apparently in the last movement of this *Te Deum*. In the 'Gloria' of his *Missa Assumpta est Maria*, also a late work, Charpentier uses 2 for 'in terra pax', then **¢**, *fort et guay*, for 'laudamus te', followed by 2, *lent*, for 'adoramus te', and **¢**, *guay*, for 'glorificamus te'; these alternations clearly confirm his view of **¢** being faster than 2.

(iii) ♩ of 3 (3/4) = ♩ of 3/2 (but see below for Charpentier's use of a variety of 3/2 notations).

(iv) relationships between duple and triple times were generally equal (♩ = ♩ or ♩ = ♩) or *sesquialtera* in character, e.g. ♩ = ♩.

The editor's suggestions for tempo relationships are indicated at appropriate points in both the Full Score and the Vocal Score.

Charpentier's varied 3/2 notations. Charpentier employed a variety of notations for that which today we would notate as 3/2. Twice in this setting of *Te Deum* (bars 277-302, 'Venerandum tuum verum' and 405-466, 'Te ergo quaesumus') he uses the mensural sign **¢** 3/2 associated with 'white' (void) notation (the original notation of Charpentier's manuscript is reproduced in facsimiles of the relevant pages in the Appendix to the Full Score). From a study of Charpentier's use of this and other notations for 3/2 time, and from the nature of the set text in these two passages, the combination of this mensural signature and void notation would seem to indicate a slow tempo.

Other performance considerations

Pitch. The pitch employed in Charpentier's day was as much as a whole tone below modern concert pitch.

Figuring of the Basse-continue. Charpentier's somewhat sparse figuring of the bass is preserved in the Full Score of this edition (although tacitly corrected in the few instances where it is misplaced or manifestly incorrect). However, in the Vocal Score and the separate *basse-continue* part it has been amplified where necessary to avoid accidents in performance. A comparison with the Full Score will always show what has been added by the editor.

Ornamentation. Charpentier only uses four ornament signs in this work, as follows:

The first two apparently indicate trills (*tremblements*) beginning on the note above, but in the second case preceded by a short staccato note at the pitch given. The third and fourth are used very sparingly; the + is a generalised ornament sign with a variety of meanings according to the context and the ⁓ apparently indicates a *pincé*, customarily preceded by a *port-de-voix*, i.e. a 'lower mordent' preceded by the note below that written:

Pronunciation. Until the early years of the twentieth century, Latin texts were sung in French churches with 'Frenchified' pronunciation, rather than the Italianate pronunciation adopted in most European countries in recent decades. Clearly, the restoration of the sound-picture of a French Baroque work by employing period instruments ought to be mirrored in the nature of the vocal sound, not least in the different vowels and consonants resulting from a Gallic pronunciation of Latin. The main characteristics of this practice are:

VOWELS: The close French 'u' as in 'sur' or 'rue' is adopted in Latin words such as 'laudamus' and 'sanctus' (where the final 's' is also sounded) and 'veneratur'; however, 'u' followed by 'm', rare in French itself, but common in Latin, in many words such as ' Deum', 'Dominum', etc., is pronounced 'om' as in the French 'tomate'; further, 'u' followed by 'n' is pronounced as the French 'un', in words such as 'sunt'. 'Au' is pronounced as in French, not as in German 'au'.

CONSONANTS: 'J' is pronounced as in the French 'je' in words such 'ejus', and 'majestatis'; 'qu' is pronounced as 'k' in words such as 'quoque' and 'quæsumus'. The 't' in the sequence 'tio' and 'tia' is pronounced more like 's' as in the French 'nation', e.g. in 'pretioso'. Before 'i' and 'e', a soft 'c' is used, so words such as 'fecit' are pronounced 'fési' (note also silent French verb endings). The 't' is silent in 'et' as in French, and 'h' is also generally silent. 'S' is also silent in words where in modern French we find either an acute or a circumflex accent (or the latter omitted) so 'nostri' is pronounced 'notri'.

Acknowledgements

The editor wishes to acknowledge permission granted by the Département de la Musique, Bibliothèque nationale de France (Directeur: Mme Catherine Massip), to reproduce four pages in facsimile, and to use Charpentier's manuscript score (Rés. Vm¹ 259, ff 73v-85) as the basis of this edition. The cover design illustration derives from an engraving in the Collections de la Bibliothèque municipale de Versailles (Conservateur-en-chef: Mme Claire Caucheteux). David Ponsford gave invaluable advice on the editorial figuring included in the Vocal Score and performing material, and John Nightingale expertly checked the practicality of the keyboard reduction and realisation. Performances of this edition in its early stages by Jeffrey Skidmore and *Ex Cathedra*, Birmingham provided valuable checks on accuracy, and led to a number of improvements in the clarity of page layout. To all of these colleagues, the editor expresses his warm thanks.

For full Introduction and Critical Report please refer to the Full Score.

Lionel Sawkins, Beckenham, 1996

Préface

Le *Te Deum* en ré majeur (H. 146) date probablement des dernières années de Charpentier, alors que celui-ci occupait le poste de maître de musique soit chez les Jésuites à Paris, (au début des années 1690), soit à la Sainte-Chapelle dans les années qui suivirent (1698-1704), où il était responsable de la musique en de nombreuses occasions de cérémonie. Il est présentée ici pour la première fois dans une édition respectant scrupuleusement les intentions du compositeur, qui figurent de façon explicite dans la claire calligraphie de la partition autographe.

Cette mise en musique, avec ses adjonctions "royales" de trompettes et timbales, s'inscrit clairement dans une tendance inaugurée par les versions de Lully en 1677 et de Lalande en 1684 : elle doit avoir été sensiblement contemporaine de celle de Purcell en 1694. De tels ouvrages ornaient presque toujours les célébrations d'action de grâce. Entre les versions festives des contemporains de Charpentier et celle-ci, la différence la plus marquante tient dans la brièveté de cette dernière: une préférence pour la concision qui a sans doute influencé Lalande, lequel réduisit en 1706 son œuvre antérieure à la moitié de ses dimensions d'origine. Des exemples quasiment contemporains, en parties séparées, pris dans l'édition imprimée du *Te Deum* de Lully en 1684, témoignent eux aussi des coupures importantes effectuées par le copiste du roi, André Danican Philidor l'aîné.

Effectif vocal

Bien que cinq solistes puissent s'avérer suffisants – deux dessus, haute contre, taille et basse – Charpentier requiert en fait un petit chœur vocal de huit chanteurs, deux par voix, et un grand chœur disposé sur ces mêmes quatre parties. (A la Sainte-Chapelle, ce groupe plus important ne comprenait lui-même, selon toute vraisemblance, que trois ou quatre chanteurs par partie du temps de Charpentier). Dans cette édition, toutes les parties de haute-contre sont notées en clé de sol dans un but de convenance, pour le cas où ces parties seraient chantées par des contre-ténors ou des altos. On utilisera toutefois de préférence des voix de ténors dans les solos de haute-contre, ainsi que dans le chœur, de façon à correspondre au son particulier souhaité par Charpentier. (Cette différence de qualité sonore mise à part, les parties de haute-contre dans la musique baroque française dépassent souvent la limite grave de l'ambitus normalement utilisé par la plupart des altos masculins ou féminins, surtout lorsque l'on adopte le diapason en usage à l'époque de Charpentier, plus bas. Cf. infra "Autres suggestions d'exécution").

Réduction pour clavier

La réduction pour clavier a également été émaillée d'indications de changement d'orchestration de façon à pouvoir être utilisée lors d'exécution accompagnées à l'orgue seul, en l'absence d'orchestre disponible. Les petites notes de la réduction de clavier indiquent la réalisation éditoriale du chiffrage. Il est utile de se souvenir que l'orgue français de ce temps ne possédait que des jeux de 8 pieds au pédalier, et que le 16 pieds n'était par conséquent pas utilisé pour la basse de l'orgue, pas plus qu'il n'était présent à l'orchestre: l'instrument le plus grave de ce dernier était la basse de violon (accordé un ton plus bas que le violoncelle).

Principes d'édition

Clés et nomenclature. Les clés d'origine sont indiquées dans la partition générale en *incipit* à la première apparition de chaque nouvelle ligne vocale ou instrumentale. La tonalité et les indications de mesure utilisées par Charpentier ont été conservées. Les secondes présentent en effet un lien significatif avec le tempo (cf. infra : "Tempo et changements de tempo") : toute modernisation aurait conduit à se priver de ces liens. Dans la partition générale, chacune des rubriques de Charpentier a été maintenue (toujours en caractère romain), et le cas échéant, étendue : toute extension est dans ce cas indiquée entre crochets (dans la partition vocale, les crochets ont été omis et les divers types de nomenclature uniformisés : les indications originales sont alors accessibles en consultant la partition générale). Les traductions ou interprétations éditoriales destinées aux lecteurs anglophones sont en *italiques*, celles destinées aux lecteurs allemands en caractères romains.

Charpentier alterne, aussi bien dans les parties vocales qu'instrumentales, les indications de solo avec la mention "Tous" (*tutti*). La ligne de basse comporte alternativement l'indication "Tous" et "Acc[ompagnement] seul", ce dernier terme étant employé pour l'accompagnement des solos ou des ensembles et correspondant à la basse-continue, c'est à dire les seuls instruments de continuo, qui comprennent ici l'orgue, la basse de viole (ou basse de violon/violoncelle) et le théorbe.

Dans la partition vocale, afin d'éviter toute confusion avec les indications générales pour les chanteurs (imprimées "TOUS"), ces autres mentions à la partie de basse sont imprimées juste au-dessus de la ligne de basse figurée (la main gauche de la réduction pour orgue) en bas de casse, "tous", en alternance avec "acc. seul".

Tempo et changements de tempo. Charpentier a numéroté les mesures d'un bout à l'autre de l'œuvre en une seule séquence, en plaçant un chiffre toutes les cent mesures, soulignant ainsi implicitement l'intégralité de la répétition du rondeau initial. La numérotation des mouvements provient en revanche de l'éditeur, et a été réalisée à la seule fin de fournir une aide lors des répétitions : elle n'entend pas impliquer de séparation entre mouvements à l'exécution, bien que, comme on pourra le constater, Charpentier demande en plusieurs endroits une pause de plus ou moins longue durée. Le fait que le compositeur ait senti nécessaire de faire figurer cette indication en clair vient nous rappeler l'usage baroque habituel de jouer de telles œuvres en continu, de "mouvement" en "mouvement", un usage que Charpentier souligne parfois dans des rubriques invitant les interprètes à enchaîner sans retard avec le mouvement suivant p. ex., "passez sans interruption à la suite".

L'existence de cette pratique nous rappelle également la nécessité de considérer la relation entre le tempo d'un "mouvement" et le suivant : de telles relations étaient alors déduites d'après la tradition de l'ancien système proportionnel, familier à tout musicien du dix-septième siècle, au travers duquel deux indications de mesure différentes étaient mises en relation proportionnelle l'une avec l'autre. Bien qu'il ne soit pas toujours facile de déterminer clairement à quelle proportion se référait Charpentier, dans cette œuvre ou dans d'autres, l'éditeur scientifique a pris ici la liberté de suggérer de plausibles relations de tempo, en se référant à d'autres œuvres de l'époque pour lesquelles des indications de durée ont été notées, ainsi qu'à des traités théoriques couramment diffusés à l'époque. La principes de base de ces relations peuvent être résumés de la sorte :

a) ♩ de **C** = ♩ de **¢** ou **2**

b) Pour la plupart des compositeurs et théoriciens en France (comme en Angleterre), **2** est le tempo le plus rapide et double souvent la vitesse de **¢** ; pour certains cependant, (dont Charpentier évidemment a fait partie) c'est l'inverse qui semble parfois avoir été le cas, avec **¢** en tempo le plus rapide, comme c'est apparemment le cas dans le dernier mouvement de ce *Te Deum*. Dans le "Gloria" de sa *Missa Assumpta est Maria*, également une œuvre tardive, Charpentier utilise **2** dans "et in terra pax", puis **¢** *fort et guay* pour "laudamus te"; suivi par **2**, *lent* pour "adoramus te", et **¢** *guay* pour "glorificamus te": ces alternances confirment nettement sa conception d'un **¢** plus

rapide que **2**.

c) ♩ de **3** (3/4) = ♩ de **3/2** (mais voir infra l'utilisation de diverses notations en **3/2** par Charpentier).

d) Les relations entre mesures binaires et ternaires étaient généralement égales (♩ = ♩ ou ♩ = ♩) ou de caractère sesquialtera, p. ex. : ♩ = ♩.

Les suggestions de l'éditeur scientifique quant aux relations de tempo sont indiquées aux endroits appropriés à la fois dans la partition générale et dans la partition vocale.

Les diverses notations 3/2 de Charpentier. Charpentier utilise une série de notations pour ce qui aujourd'hui serait noté en **3/2**. A deux reprises dans cette version du *Te Deum* (mesures 277-302, "Venerandum tuum verum" et 405-466, "Te ergo quaesumus") il utilise le signe de mesure **¢ 3/2** en l'associant à la notation "blanche" (la notation originale dans le manuscrit de Charpentier est reproduite en facsimilé des pages concernées dans l'Appendice de la partition générale). Une étude de l'usage que fait Charpentier de cette notation particulière et des autres notations de la mesure à **3/2**, ainsi que la nature du texte mis en musique dans ces deux passages, la combinaison de l'indication de mesure et de la notation blanche, sont autant d'éléments qui sembleraient indiquer un tempo lent.

Autres suggestions d'exécution

Diapason. Le diapason en usage à l'époque de Charpentier était situé vers un ton entier au-dessous du diapason moderne.

Réalisation de la Basse-continue. La réalisation quelque peu parcimonieuse de la basse par Charpentier est conservée dans la partition générale de la présente édition (bien que corrigée implicitement sur les quelques passages où celle-ci apparaît mal placée ou manifestement incorrecte). Dans la partition vocale ainsi que dans la partie séparée de basse-continue toutefois, elle a été développée partout où cela s'avérait nécessaire afin d'éviter tout accroc lors de l'exécution. Une comparaison avec la partition générale permettra d'avoir toujours en vue les ajouts dus à l'éditeur scientifique.

Ornementation. Charpentier n'utilise que quatre signes d'ornement dans son œuvre, ce sont :

Les deux premiers indiquent apparemment des trilles (tremblements) débutant à la note supérieure, mais précédé par une courte note *staccato* sur la hauteur donnée dans le second cas. Les troisième et quatrième sont utilisés de façon très économe: le + est un ornement d'emploi général comportant une grande variété de réalisations en fonction du contexte, le ⚹ indique apparemment un pincé, habituellement précédé d'un port-de-voix, il s'agit, en d'autres termes d'un "mordant inférieur" précédé par la note inférieure de la note écrite:

Prononciation. Jusqu'aux premières années du XXe siècle, les textes latins étaient chantés dans les églises françaises dans une prononciation "francisée", plutôt que dans la prononciation italienne adoptée par la suite dans la plupart des pays européens. Il est clair que la restitution de l'image sonore d'une œuvre baroque française effectuée grâce au recours aux instruments anciens doit également se refléter dans la nature du son vocal, tout au moins dans les différentes voyelles et consonnes résultant d'une prononciation du latin à la française. Les principales caractéristiques de cette pratique sont les suivantes :

VOYELLES: le "u" fermé français de "sur" ou "rue" est adopté dans des mots latins "laudamus" et "sanctus" (où la finale "s" est également prononcée) et "veneratur" ; le "u" suivis du "m", rare en français, mais fréquent en latin, dans de nombreux mots comme "Deum" "Dominum", etc. se prononce "om" comme dans "tomate" ; "u" suivi de "n" est en outre prononcé comme dans le français "un", dans des mots comme "sunt". "Au" est prononcé comme en français, et non comme dans l'allemand "au".

CONSONNES: "j" se prononce comme en français "je", dans des mots tels que "ejus" et "majestatis" ; "qu" se prononce "k" dans des mots comme "quoque" et "quaesumus". Le "t" des groupements "tio" et "tia" se rapproche davantage d'un "s" comme dans le français "nation", p. ex. dans "pretioso". Avant "i" et "e" on emploie le "c" sifflant, de sort que des mots comme "fecit" se prononcent "fési" (où l'on observe également la terminaison muette des verbes français). Le "t" est muet dans "et" comme en français, ce qui est généralement aussi le cas du "h". "S" est également muet dans des mots où nous trouvons en français moderne des accents aigu ou circonflexe, de sorte que "nostri" par exemple se prononce "notri".

Remerciements

Au Département de la Musique, Bibliothèque Nationale de France (Directeur : Mme Catherine Massip), l'éditeur scientifique souhaite adresser l'expression de sa reconnaisance, pour la permission qui lui a été donnée de reproduire quatre pages en fac-similé, et d'utiliser la partition manuscrite de Charpentier (Rés. Vm^1 259, ff. 73v-85) comme base de la présente édition. L'illustration de couverture a été conçue d'après une gravure conservée dans les Collections de la Bibliothèque Municipale de Versailles (Conservateur-en-chef : Mme Claire Caucheteux). David Ponsford fut d'un conseil inappréciable quant au chiffrage éditorial inclus dans la partition vocale et le matériel d'exécution, John Nightingale vérifia de façon experte la conformité pratique de la réduction et de la réalisation au clavier. Des exécutions réalisées à partir de cette édition, alors qu'elle n'en était qu'à ses premiers développements, par Jeffrey Skidmore et *Ex Cathedra*, à Birmingham, se sont révélées des expériences de grand profit pour en tester la validité: elles conduisirent à un certain nombre d'améliorations quant à la clarté de la mise en page. A tous ces collègues, l'éditeur scientifique adresse ses chaleureux remerciements.

Pour l'introduction complète et le commentaire critique, veuillez vous référer à la partition générale.

Lionel Sawkins, Beckenham, 1996

Vorwort

Das *Te Deum* in D-dur (H. 146) entstand vermutlich in Charpentiers letzten Lebensjahren, entweder während seiner Wirkungszeit als *maître de musique* am Jesuitenkolleg in Paris in der frühen 1690er Jahren oder zwischen 1698-1704, als er eine ähnliche Position an der Sainte-Chapelle bekleidete; in diesem Amt war er für die musikalische Ausgestaltung zahlreicher zeremonieller Anlässe verantwortlich. Das Werk ist eines von vier überlieferten *Te Deum*-Vertonungen des Komponisten und liegt hier erstmals in einer Ausgabe vor, die genau den im Autograph mit seinem außerordentlich schönen und klaren Schriftbild deutlich werdenden Vorstellungen Charpentiers folgt.

Dieses Werk mit seiner für 'königliche' Anlässe üblichen großen Besetzung mit Trompeten und Pauken ist im Zusammenhang mit den *Te Deum*-Vertonungen von Lully (1677) sowie Lalande (1684) zu sehen; außerdem steht es in enger zeitlicher Nachbarschaft zu Purcells *Te Deum* von 1694. Kompositionen dieser Art waren hauptsächlich zur musikalischen Untermalung Danksagungsfeierlichkeiten bestimmt. Charpentiers *Te Deum* ist wesentlich kürzer gefaßt als die bereits oben erwähnten Werke seiner Zeitgenossen - möglicherweise sah sich Lalande durch dieses Beispiel genötigt, seine eigene Vertonung im Jahre 1706 um die Hälfte einzukürzen. Aus der gleichen Zeit stammen einige Stimmbücher des 1684 veröffentlichten Drucks von Lullys *Te Deum*. In ihnen nahm der königliche Kopist, André Danican Philidor *l'aîné*.

Singstimmen

Obwohl eine Besetzung mit fünf Solisten eigentlich ausreichend wäre – jeweils zwei *dessus* (Sopran), *haute-contre* (hoher Tenor bzw. Alt), *taille* (Tenor), und *basse* (Baß) – schreibt Charpentier einen *petit chœur* mit acht Sängern vor, jede Stimme ist also doppelt besetzt. (Wahrscheinlich waren die Partien in Charpentiers Zeit an der Sainte-Chapelle sogar drei- bis vierfach besetzt). In der vorliegenden Ausgabe wurden die *haute-contre*-Stimmen im Violinschlüssel notiert, um bei Besetzung mit Countertenören oder Altisten eine angenehmere Lesart zu bieten. Wenn irgend möglich sollten für den Solostellen jedoch Tenöre eingesetzt werden, auch in den Chören, um Charpentiers angestrebten Klangbild möglichst nahe zu kommen. (Abgesehen von der Frage des unterschiedlichen Klangcharakters liegen die *haute-contre*-Partien des französischen Barock außerdem im Grenzbereich vieler Altisten bzw. Altistinnen, besonders wenn man in der zu Charpentiers Zeiten üblichen tieferen Stimmung spielt; siehe hierzu auch 'Weitere Hinweise zur Ausführung').

Klavierauszug

Die jeweiligen Besetzungsänderungen sind zusätzlich im Klavierauszug angegeben, als Hilfe bei Aufführungen, in denen kein Orchester zur Verfügung steht und nur die Orgel die Begleitung übernimmt. Bei den kleingedruckten Noten in der Klavierauszug handelt es sich um Zusätze des Herausgebers. Außerdem ist anzumerken, daß das Pedalwerk der französischen Orgeln der Zeit nur 8'-Pfeifen aufwies, 16'-Lagen finden sich also im Orgelbaß nicht, auch nicht im Orchester selbst, dessen tiefstes Instrument die einen Ton tiefer als das Cello gestimmte *basse de violon* war.

Editorische Vorgehensweise

Schlüssel und Nomenklatur. Die originalen Schlüssel werden zu Beginn jeder Vokal- bzw. Instrumentalstimme in Incipits wiedergegeben, die von Charpentier verwendeten Tonarten- und Taktbezeichnungen wurden beibehalten. Letztere haben eine spezifische Bedeutung für das jeweilige Tempo (siehe unten: 'Tempo und Tempobeziehungen'), eine Modernisierung würde diese Wechselbeziehungen verschleiern. In der Partitur wurden Charpentiers Bezeichnungen in normaler, nicht-kursiver Schrift wiedergegeben und, wo es notwendig erschien, ergänzt; alle Ergänzungen erscheinen in eckigen Klammern. (Im Klavierauszug wurden diese Klammern ausgelassen, die Nomenklatur wurde vereinheitlicht; die originalen Angaben lassen sich im Vergleich mit der Partitur ermitteln). Übersetzungen oder Übertragungen des Herausgebers sind für englischsprachige Benutzer in kursiver, für deutsche in nicht-kursiver Schrift wiedergegeben. Fußnoten des Herausgebers erscheinen in kursiver, Charpentiers Angaben dagegen in nicht-kursiver Schrift.

In Vokal- wie Instrumentalstimmen setzt Charpentier die tutti-Abschnitte mit dem Vermerk 'Tous' von den Solopassagen ab. Die Baßstimme ist wechselweise mit 'Tous' bzw. 'Acc[ompagnement] seul' bezeichnet; letztere Angabe findet sich bei der Begleitung von Soli und Ensembles, die hier nur vom *basse-continue*, d. h. nur mit der Continuogruppe mit Orgel, Baßgambe (oder *basse de violon*/Cello) und Theorbe bestritten wird.

Um Verwechslungen mit den allgemeinen Bezeichnungen für die Sänger (als 'TOUS' wiedergegeben) zu vermeiden, wurden die sich nur auf die Baßstimme beziehenden Angaben im Klavierauszug in Kleinbuchstaben unmittelbar über der Generalbaßstimme abgedruckt, 'tous' im Wechsel mit 'acc. seul'.

Tempo und Tempobeziehungen. Charpentier nummerierte die Takte in seinem Werk in einer Folge durch, wobei er Taktzahlen für jeden hundertsten Takt angab. Diese Zählung ist ein Indiz dafür, daß auch die Wiederholung des Eröffnungsrondeaus als notwendiger Bestandteil in das Werk eingebunden ist. Die Taktzählung in den einzelnen Sätzen ist ein editorischer Zusatz, der lediglich zur schnelleren Orientierung während der Proben dient. Damit soll keine Unterteilung in verschiedene Sätze suggeriert werden, obwohl Charpentier an mehreren Stellen längere oder kürzere Pausen zwischen den einzelnen Abschnitten verlangt. Die Tatsache, daß er diese

Angaben überhaupt für notwendig hielt, ist ein Beleg für die barocke Praxis, Werke dieser Art 'Satz' für 'Satz' in einem Zug zu spielen; darauf verweist auch sein an manchen Punkten angegebener Vermerk, die Sätze unmittelbar ineinander übergehen zu lassen, 'passez sans interruption à la suite' ('ohne Pause zum nächsten Satz weiter').

Vor dem Hintergrund dieser Praxis sind außerdem die Beziehungen zwischen den Tempi der einzelnen 'Sätze' von großer Wichtigkeit; die unterschiedlichen Tempoverhältnisse ließen sich mit Hilfe des alten Mensuralnotationsprinzips festlegen, einer Notationsart, die allen Musikern des 17. Jahrhunderts bekannt war und in dem das Verhältnis der Taktarten zueinander durch verschiedene Proportionen geregelt war.

Die von Charpentier gewünschten Proportionen in diesem wie in anderen Werken lassen sich nicht immer exakt ermitteln. Auf der Grundlage von Vergleichen mit anderen Kompositionen, in denen die Verhältnisse genauer angegeben sind, sowie weit verbreiteten theoretischen Abhandlungen der Zeit hat der Herausgeber sich jedoch erlaubt, die wohl wahrscheinlichsten Tempoverhältnisse vorzuschlagen. Die Grundprinzipien dieser Beziehungen stellen sich wie folgt dar:

(i) ♩ in **C** = ♪ in ₵ oder **2**

(ii) Für die meisten Komponisten und Theoretiker in Frankreich wie in England galt **2** als schnellstes Tempo, oftmals doppelt so schnell wie ₵; dennoch finden sich auch bei Charpentier selbst genau gegensätzliche Fälle, d. h. ₵ gab das schnellste Tempo an, wie im letzten Satz seines *Te Deum*. Im 'Gloria' von Charpentiers *Missa Assumpta est Maria*, ein Werk, das ebenfalls in seinen letzten Lebensjahren entstand, benutzt er für den Abschnitt 'in terra pax' die Vorzeichnung **2**, dann ₵, *fort et guay* für den Abschnitt 'laudamus te', gefolgt von **2**, *lent*, für das 'adoramus te', sowie ₵, *guay*, für 'glorificamus te'; diese verschiedenen Abstufungen belegen eindeutig, daß das Zeichen ₵ bei Charpentier ein schnelleres Tempo anzeigt als **2**.

(iii) ♩ in **3** (3/4) = ♪ in **3/2** (vgl. jedoch Kommentare zu Charpentiers verschiedene von 3/2-Notationsweisen)

(iv) Die Verhältnisse zwischen Abschnitten mit Zweier- bzw. Dreiermensuren blieben entweder bestehen (♩ = ♩ oder ♩ = ♪), oder es lag die proportio sesquialtera vor, d. h. ♩ = ♩.

Die Angaben des Herausgebers bezüglich der Tempoverhältnisse sind in der Partitur sowie dem Klavierauszug an den relevanten Stellen vermerkt.

Charpentiers verschiedene 3/2-Notationsweisen. Charpentier verwendete eine Vielzahl von Vorzeichnungen für Verhältnisse, die wir heute als **3/2** notieren würden. An zwei Stellen in seinem *Te Deum* (Takte 277-302, 'Venerandum tuum verum' und 405-466, 'Te ergo quaesumus') benutzt er das Mensurzeichen ₵ **3/2** in Verbindung mit weißer Notation (die entsprechenden Abschnitte sind im Faksimile im Anhang zur Partitur wiedergegeben).

Charpentiers Verwendung dieser sowie anderer Notationsweisen für **3/2**-Taktarten in anderen Werken, sowie der jeweilige Textcharakter dieser Abschnitte lassen darauf schließen, daß die Kombination dieses Mensurzeichens mit weißer Notation auf ein langsames Tempo hinweist.

Weitere Hinweise zur Ausführung

Stimmung. Die Stimmung eines Orchesters zu Charpentiers Zeit lag bis zu einem Ganzton unter der heute üblichen Stimmung.

Bezifferung des Basse-continue. Charpentiers originale, sparsame Generalbaßbezifferung wurde in der Partitur dieser Ausgabe abgedruckt (obwohl an einigen Stellen stillschweigend Korrekturen vorgenommen wurden, wo die Ziffern nicht korrekt unter der entsprechenden Note standen, oder eindeutige Fehler vorlagen). Im Klavierauszug und dem separaten *basse-continue* wurden die Stimmen, wo es notwendig erschien, aufgefüllt, um Fehler bei der Ausführung zu vermeiden. Im Vergleich mit der Partitur werden die Zusätze des Herausgebers jedoch deutlich.

Verzierungen. Charpentier verwendet nur vier Verzierungs-

zeichen in diesem Werk, wie folgt:

ᵂᵂ ·ᵂᵂ + ᶬᵂ

Die ersten zwei Zeichen stehen für Triller (*tremblements*), die einen Ton über der jeweiligen Note beginnen, im zweiten Fall jedoch geht eine kurze staccato-Note in der notierten Tonhöhe voraus. Das dritte und vierte Zeichen erscheint nur selten. Das + deutet nur allgemein eine Verzierung an, deren genauere Bedeutung von dem jeweiligen Zusammenhang abhängt, in dem es erscheint; das ᶬᵂ bezeichnet ein *pincé*, dem normalerweise ein *port-de-voix* vorangestellt ist, d. h. ein Mordent, der einen Ton unter der angegebenen Note beginnt: ♪♫

Aussprache. Bis zum Beginn des 20. Jahrhunderts war es im französischen Kirchengesang üblich, lateinische Texte in ihrer Aussprache dem Französischen anzugleichen, man folgte nicht der italianisierten Form, wie sie in den letzten Jahrzehnten in den meisten europäischen Ländern üblich geworden ist. Wenn man sich um ein möglichst getreues Abbild des Klanges eines französischen Musikwerks des Barocks bemüht, sollten natürlich auch die Vokalstimmen mit bedacht werden. Dies gilt besonders für die Ausprache der verschiedenen Vokale und Konsonanten, die sich natürlich durch die Angleichung des lateinischen Textes an den französischen Duktus Verändert. Die wichtigsten Kennzeichen dieser Praxis sind:

VOKALE: Das geschlossene französische 'u' wie in 'sur' oder 'rue' findet auch in lateinischen Worten wie 'laudamus' oder 'sanctus' (in dem auch das letzte 's' mitgesprochen wird) und 'veneratur' Verwendung; die im Französischen relativ seltene, im Lateinischen jedoch häufig anzutreffende Folge 'u' und 'm' in Worten wie 'Deum', 'Dominum' etc. wird 'om' wie in 'tomate' ausgesprochen, das 'u' gefolgt von einem 'n' in Worten wie 'sunt' entspricht dem französischen 'un'. 'Au' ist in französischer Manier auszusprechen, nicht wie das deutsche 'au'.

KONSONANTEN: 'J' wird wie im französischen 'je' ausgesprochen, etwa bei 'ejus' und 'majestatis'; in Worten wie 'quoque' und 'quaesumus' entspricht das 'qu' in der Aussprache dem 'k'. Das 't' in der Folge 'tio' und 'tia' wird ähnlich wie das 's' im französischen 'nation' ausgesprochen, so in 'pretioso'. Vor 'i' und 'e' steht ein weiches 'c', Worte wie 'fecit' sollten daher 'fési' ausgesprochen werden (man beachte auch die stummen Endungen der französischen Verben). Wie im französischen 'et' wird das 't' nicht mitgesprochen; dies gilt in den meisten Fällen auch für das 'h'. Außerdem wird 's' in Worten, bei denen wir im modernen Französisch einen accent aigu oder circonflexe schreiben (oder letzterer ausfällt) nicht mitgesprochen, 'nostri' sollte daher wie 'notri' klingen.

Danksagungen

Der Herausgeber bedankt sich für die Abdruckgenehmigung des Départements de la musique der Bibliothèque nationale de France (Directeur: Mme Catherine Massip) der vier Faksimileseiten, sowie für die Erlaubnis, Charpentiers autographe Partitur, die die Grundlage dieser Notenausgabe bildet (Rés. Vm^1 259, ff. 73v-85), einsehen zu dürfen. Als Vorlage für das Cover diente ein Stich aus der Sammlung der Bibliothéque municipale de Versailles (Conservateur-en-chef: Mme Claire Caucheteux). David Ponsford ist für seine unschätzbare Hilfe bezüglich der Bezifferungen im Klavierauszug sowie im Aufführungsmaterial zu danken, John Nightingale prüfte die Spielbarkeit des Klavierauszugs sowie die Aussetzung. Aufführungen des Werkes mit *Ex Cathedra*, Birmingham, unter Leitung von Jeffrey Skidmore, für die die vorliegende noch in ihrer Entstehungsphase befindliche Ausgabe herangezogen wurde, erlaubten nochmalige Überprüfungen und führten zu weiteren Verbesserungen hinsichtlich der Klarheit des Layouts. Allen diesen Kollegen sei vom Herausgeber herzlichst gedankt.

Für eine detaillierte Einführung sowie den Kritischen Bericht sei auf die Partitur des Werkes verwiesen.

Lionel Sawkins, Beckenham, 1996

Te Deum

MARC-ANTOINE CHARPENTIER, H.146
edited by Lionel Sawkins

1	*Prélude*			1
2	*Basse* : Te Deum laudamus, te Dominum confitemur.	*We praise thee, O God: we acknowledge thee to be the Lord.*	Dieu, nous te louons; Seigneur, nous te glorifions.	2
3	*Grand Chœur* : Te aeternum patrem omnis terra veneratur. Tibi omnes angeli, tibi caeli et universae potestates. *Quatuor (2 Dessus, Haute-Contre, Taille)*: Tibi cherubim et seraphim incessabili voce proclamant: Sanctus, sanctus, sanctus, Dominus Deus sabaoth.	*All the earth doth worship thee, the Father everlasting. To thee all angels cry aloud, the heavens and all the powers therein.* *To thee Cherubim and Seraphim continually do cry: Holy, holy, holy, Lord God of Sabaoth.*	Père éternel, la terre entière te revère. A toi, tous les anges, les cieux, et les puissances de l'univers. A toi, Chérubins et Séraphins proclament d'une voix ininterrompue: Saint, saint, saint, Seigneur, Dieu des armées.	3
4	*Grand Chœur* : Pleni sunt caeli et terra majestatis gloriae tuae. Te gloriosus apostolorum chorus, te prophetarum laudabilis numerus, te martyrum candidatus laudat exercitus.	*Heaven and earth are full of the majesty of thy glory. The glorious company of the apostles, the goodly fellowship of the prophets, the noble army of martyrs praise thee.*	Les cieux et la terre sont remplis de la majesté de ta gloire. Le chœur glorieux des apôtres, la troupe vénérable des prophètes, la blanche armée des martyrs te louent.	7
5	*Duo (Haute-Contre, Taille)* : Te per orbem terrarum sancta confitetur ecclesia, Patrem immensae majestatis, Venerandum tuum verum et unicum Filium. *Trio (Haute-Contre, Taille, Basse)* : Sanctum quoque paraclitum Spiritum. Tu rex gloriae, Christe, Tu Patris sempiternus es Filius. Tu ad liberandum suscepturus hominem non horruisti virginis uterum.	*The holy church throughout all the world doth acknowledge thee, the Father of an infinite majesty, thy true and only Son, worthy of honour.* *The Holy Spirit, the comforter. Thou art the king of glory, O Christ, thou art the everlasting Son of the Father. When thou tookest upon thee to deliver man, thou didst not abhor the Virgin's womb.*	Par toute la terre la sainte église témoigne de toi. Père d'immense majesté, ton vrai et unique Fils digne de vénération. Aussi, l'Esprit Saint consolateur. Tu es le roi de gloire, Christ. Tu es le Fils éternel du Père. Résolu à délivrer l'homme, tu n'as pas craint le sein d'une vierge.	11
6	*Grand Chœur* : Tu devicto mortis aculeo aperuisti credentibus regna caelorum. Tu ad dexteram Dei sedes in gloria Patris. *Basse* : Judex crederis esse venturus.	*Overcoming the sharpness of death, thou didst open the kingdom of heaven to all believers. Thou sittest at the right hand of God, in the glory of the Father.* *We believe that thou shalt come to be our judge.*	Ayant vaincu l'aiguillon de la mort, tu as ouvert aux croyants le royaume des cieux. Tu es assis à la droite de Dieu, dans la gloire du Père. Nous croyons que tu viendras comme juge.	15
7	*Dessus* : Te ergo quaesumus, tuis famulis subveni, quos pretioso sanguine redemisti.	*We beseech thee, therefore, help thy servants, whom thou hast redeemed by thy precious blood.*	Toi, donc, nous le demandons, viens au secours de tes serviteurs que tu as rachetés par ton sang précieux.	17
8	*Petit Chœur & Grand Chœur* : Aeterna fac cum sanctis tuis in gloria numerari. Salvum fac populum tuum Domine et benedic hereditati tuae, et rege eos et extolle illos usque in aeternum. Per singulos dies benedicimus te, et laudamus nomen tuum in saeculum et in saeculum saeculi.	*Make them to be numbered with thy saints, in glory everlasting. O Lord, save thy people, and bless thine heritage; govern them and lift them up for ever. Day by day we bless thee, and praise thy name for evermore..*	Qu'il soient comptés parmi les saints dans la gloire éternelle. Sauve ton peuple, Seigneur, et bénis ton héritage. Et gouverne-le et protège-le jusqu'à l'éternité. Chaque jour nous te bénissons, et nous louons ton nom à jamais dans les siècles des siècles.	19
9	*Duo (Dessus, Basse)* : Dignare Domine die isto sine peccato nos custodire. Miserere nostri, Domine, miserere nostri.	*Grant, O Lord, to keep us this day without sin. Have mercy upon us O Lord, have mercy upon us.*	Daigne, Seigneur, en ce jour nous préserver de tout péché. Aie pitié de nous, Seigneur, aie pitié de nous.	23
10	*Trio (2 Dessus, Basse)*: Fiat misericordia tua Domine super nos, quemadmodum speravimus in te.	*Let thy mercy, O Lord, lighten upon us, as our trust is in thee.*	Que ta miséricorde, Seigneur, soit sur nous selon l'espérance que nous avons mise en toi.	25
11	*Petit Chœur & Grand Chœur* : In te Domine speravi, non confundar in aeternum.	*In thee, O Lord, have I trusted: let me never be confounded.*	En toi, Seigneur, j'ai espéré; que je ne sois point confondu à jamais.	27

Te Deum, H.146

Edited by Lionel Sawkins

MARC-ANTOINE CHARPENTIER

1. Prélude

2. Te Deum laudamus

te Do - mi - num, te De - um, te Do - mi - num, te Do - mi - num con - fi -

te - mur, te Do - mi - num, te Do - mi - num con - fi - te - mur.

Suivez après une petite pause
Continue after a brief pause
Nach kleiner Pause weiter

3. Te aeternum Patrem

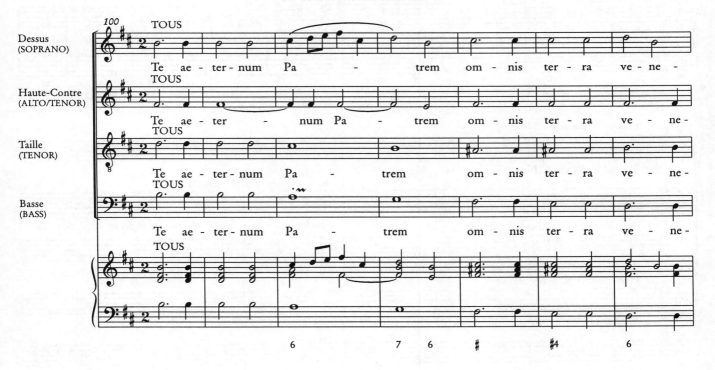

Dessus (SOPRANO)
TOUS
Te ae - ter - num Pa - trem om - nis ter - ra ve - ne -

Haute-Contre (ALTO/TENOR)
TOUS
Te ae - ter - num Pa - trem om - nis ter - ra ve - ne -

Taille (TENOR)
TOUS
Te ae - ter - num Pa - trem om - nis ter - ra ve - ne -

Basse (BASS)
TOUS
Te ae - ter - num Pa - trem om - nis ter - ra ve - ne -

6

4. Pleni sunt caeli

8

10

12

* Cet ancien signe de mesure, utilisé ici (& aux m. 405-446) avec la notation blanche, semble indiquer un tempo assez lent (voir la préface).
La notation originale se trouve dans l'Appendix de la partition générale. *This time-signature, used here (and in bars 405-446) in conjunction
with void notation, apparently indicates a slow tempo (see preface). The original notation is reproduced in the Appendix to the full score.*
Diese Mensurvorzeichnung steht hier (und ebenso in den Takten 405-446) in Verbindung mit 'weißer Notation'. Offensichtlich wird damit
ein langsames Tempo angezeigt (vgl. das Vorwort). Das originale Notenbild ist im 'Appendix' von der Partitur wiedergegeben.

14

Passez sans interruption à la suite
Continue uninterrupted to the next movement
Ohne Pause weiter

6. Tu devicto

7. Récit: Te ergo quaesumus

* Voir la note, page 12. *See footnote, page 12.* Siehe Anmerkung auf Seite 12.

18

Suivez au Chœur sans interruption
Follow on to the chorus without interruption
Nach dem Chor ohne Pause weiter

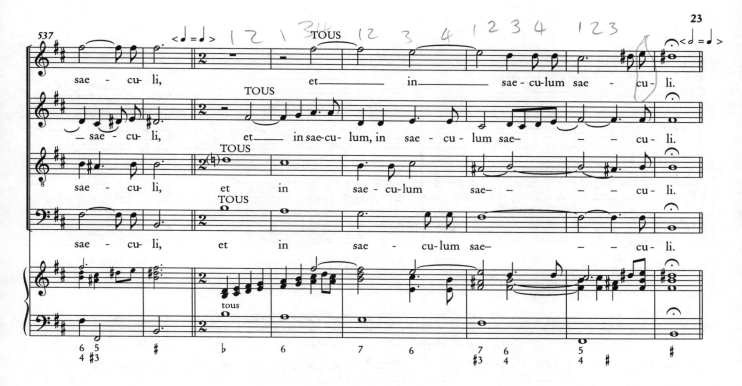

Suivez après un grand silence
Continue after a long silence
Nach langer Pause weiter

9. Duo: Dignare

10. Trio: Fiat misericordia

26

Suivez après un peu de silence au dernier couplet
Continue with the last verse after a short silence
Nach kurzer Pause zum letzten Couplet

11. In te Domine

28

32